Silent Grief:

Hope for Surviving Early Miscarriage

By

Kendra D. Graber

Silent Grief

Text copyright © 2015 Kendra D. Graber

ISBN-13: 978-0996365604

ISBN-10: 0996365605

Truth in Word Publishing, LLC

1444 Homestead Loop

Bonners Ferry, ID 83805

www.truthinwordpublishing.com

Contact publisher for special quantity discounts.

Silent Grief is dedicated to these women who have survived early miscarriages, and were brave enough to share their stories with us:

Michelle

Melissa Cummins

Lacey

Tina Zimmerman

Joanna Yoder

Robin

Savannah Berniquez

Fay D.

Racheal Heath

Ruthann M.

Kristina

Louise F.

Lois Troyer

Noel

. . . and to my Lord and Savior Jesus Christ – whom I seek to honor with my life.

Table of Contents

Introduction 7

My Story 11

Life as God Sees It: The Biblical Principle of
Life Within the Womb 29

From The Depths of Grief 37

The Day That Never Was 43

The Practical Side of Miscarriage 51

Their Stories 63

For Those Looking On 109

Grieving Silently No Longer 120

Introduction

Why would a woman ever wish to write about miscarriage? Why, when it's been years down the road, would she want to submerge herself in the pain of those days once again? Wouldn't it be better to leave well enough alone – to not touch the grief of those long-gone days, but let them lay in the past where they belong?

I've thought these questions while deciding whether or not to write this book. But I could not shake the feeling that God would have me do it. **That He brought me through the journey of early miscarriage not only for my own sake, but for the sake of others.**

The Scar

The wound – it was a sorry sight – so ugly,
red, and bruised.

The blood spilled out and over as pain went
coursing through.

In agony, I cried "Oh God, will this wound
never heal?"

Until I saw the miracle His finger did reveal.

As over time His loving hand worked
wonders in my heart.

And closed the wound – that gaping
wound – which did so sting and smart.

But to bring healing to the wound **He had to leave a scar**.

And then I prayed, "Oh Lord, it shall remind me who You are.

It'll teach me of the love it took for You to die for me.

It's a shadow of the scar You bore to set my lost soul free."

And as someday down the road of life, I turn my head to find -

A wounded heart that's bleeding . . . then this scar shall come to mind.

"Oh God!" I'll cry, "I then shall know Your

reason for my pain.

For from this scar shall come Your healing

that will be my brother's gain."

And so this is the reason why I pick
up my pen and write . . .

Kendra

My Story

I could feel the hard table beneath me as I lay in the ultrasound room. Fear's icy grip held my heart, squeezing it tighter and tighter.

The ultrasound technician ran the wand over my belly. Looking.

Minutes ticked by. And nothing was said.

"Please!" I wanted to scream. "Tell me you see something!" Where is that precious tiny heartbeat that should be flickering on the screen? Shouldn't I be hearing a little thumping cadence coming from the speaker? But I couldn't see the screen since the technician had discreetly turned it away.

More minutes inched painfully past as she slowly moved her wand again. Still, she said nothing.

Dread settled into the pit of my stomach – as though I knew what the answer would be. Setting the wand down, she turned the screen even further away and walked to the door. Said she would have to go get the doctor.

That's when I knew.

I knew my baby had gone Home. I knew that there was no little heartbeat on the screen, or inside my womb. It had been snuffed out – almost before it had started.

Nine weeks I had held this precious baby inside me. Nine extremely short weeks.

In the silence of that room, I came face to face with reality. The reality that leaves you feeling cold, dead, and so very alone. The reality that I now carried only the shell of a baby inside me. My sweet baby that had taken wings and flown to heaven . . . leaving me alone.

The reality of it all took my breath away. And I had to somehow get a handle on my emotions before the doctor walked back in the door. Tears rushed to the surface as all I wanted was to go home, curl up in my bed, and cry until there were no tears left.

But there were footsteps sounding in the hallway now.

The doctor came in, picked up the wand, and looked once more. Nothing. Things became a blur as he told me I was probably having a threatened miscarriage since he had seen no heart activity, and mechanically handed me my lab papers.

It felt so cold. There was no explanation of what might have happened or sympathy for my grief that threatened to engulf me. Nothing but the cold papers in my hand, sending me to the lab for confirmation that my little one had surely died.

Somehow I stumbled out to my car, tears blinding my eyes. What in the world had happened? And how was I supposed to deal with it?

I was a newlywed, having only been married ten months before. Life was all still rose petals and daffodils.

Nobody I knew had ever had a miscarriage. Nobody had warned me this could happen. Nothing had prepared me for the breathtaking grief that losing such a tiny being could invoke.

I felt so alone. Although I knew my husband cared, I still felt incredibly alone. Almost like a part of my heart had died. Somebody that had been with me everywhere I went for nine short weeks had been suddenly ripped away.

And I was left feeling wide open, vulnerable, and hurting.

◊ ◊ ◊

Time has a way of healing broken hearts. I did indeed lose that sweet baby. And I grieved for her like I'd never grieved before. She deserved a time of mourning, for she was a precious angel who had fluttered in and out of my life for too short a time.

Five more months passed. Months in which I learned the awful facts of miscarriage and the medical field.

I spent those five months researching the internet on the causes of miscarriage. When I had lost my baby, I also was told that the medical field does not begin to do any testing for miscarriage until a woman has lost three babies.

I was stunned. Three miscarriages? I didn't think my heart could take two more of the experience I had just come through before finding out the reason why.

While I greatly admire the medical field, this began to peel away the rosy glasses in which I viewed my doctors. Perhaps they didn't know everything. Perhaps I could help myself. And that's just what I did.

After researching and reading for hours on end, I became convinced that I showed symptoms of low progesterone. This is a common cause of early miscarriage, and I was determined to at least rule it out before losing another baby.

When the results of my hormone test came back, I was delighted to find out that my suspicions were correct! Delighted might be a strange word to use when referring to this topic, but you must understand something here. There is nothing more discouraging than feeling helpless in the face of miscarriage.

And helpless was how I felt until I could figure out the reason why I had lost my baby – and what to do about it. With low progesterone, the remedy is fairly simple and often cures it. So I began supplementing with natural progesterone cream, as well as taking herbs that regulated hormones.

Then I found out I was pregnant again.

If you've ever been pregnant following a miscarriage, you will know how I felt. The joy that had been there with the first pregnancy was there, but it was tempered by a mountain of fear.

I held my breath and waited. Would I lose this baby too?

Sadly, I didn't have to wait long. At six weeks a second sweet baby went Home to Jesus. And I was left with empty arms. Again.

It wasn't fair. It simply wasn't fair.

Other women had babies left and right with no problems whatsoever. What was wrong with my body that made it so I couldn't sustain a pregnancy? Why did I have to keep losing babies?

I had barely gotten over dealing with my first miscarriage. How in the world could I deal with another?

Sundays were the hardest. I would go to church and see the ladies with small babies or those with rounding pregnant bellies – and I could hardly stem the tears that wanted to flow. I could feel the pity from those who knew of my loss. But I didn't want pity. I simply wanted my baby back.

Yet in the midst of my grief, a tiny glimmer of hope remained. I knew that what I was doing to help support and regulate my hormones would take time, so a second miscarriage wasn't a complete and total surprise. I had researched enough to know that it could take many months for my body to get to where it needed to be in order to keep a baby alive and healthy.

So I kept on with my natural supplements. And I kept reading. I was convinced that information was vital in me learning how to help my body in the healing process.

Two more months passed.

Then I held in my hand a test with two pink lines.

Excitement crept into my heart, threatening to crowd out the fear that resided there. I wanted this baby so much! Would my body have healed enough to let me finally hold a baby in my arms?

Hours turned into days. Days turned into weeks. Three weeks to be exact.

And then the awful spotting began.

My heart plummeted to my toes. Not again! "Oh God, I cannot deal with this again!" Just when I had begun to hope that my body would sustain a pregnancy – now I might be asked to give up yet another baby.

I did what almost every miscarriage article said to do when you begin spotting. I lay down, put my feet up, and called my doctor. Dialing his number, I looked out the window at the bright blue sky. Not really seeing it. And as I waited for the nurse to answer, it hit me.

I felt different.

This time I had the **most distinct feeling that my baby was still alive**. Although it has been fourteen years, I can still remember that beautiful feeling! I had the classic sign of a threatening miscarriage and facts pointed to this baby dying too . . . yet another feeling was taking root inside my heart.

The feeling of life within me. A new life that refused to be snuffed out.

Hope burgeoned within my breast as we did what we'd done the previous times. We waited. However, this time was different. Because my new doctor was aware of my low progesterone, he quickly put me on a strong dose of progestin.

Then he asked me to come in for an ultrasound. Memories of the previous one came rushing back. The cold, hard table. The silent technician. The screen with no flickering heartbeat. The speakers that only gave the sound of static – no beautiful, rhythmic cadence.

I didn't know if I could take it.

This time, I didn't go in alone. My husband went with me. Holding my breath, I kept my eyes on the technician's face – trying to gauge what she was seeing on the screen. "Please tell me you see a heartbeat! Please." But the words couldn't make it past my icy lips.

Then she turned the screen toward me with a big smile. "Here is your baby! And there is his heart beating!"

My breath caught. **My baby?**

Looking at the screen, I couldn't hold myself together anymore. There on that black and white screen was my baby with his little heart beating for all it was worth! He was really and actually alive!

Then my heart did a double take. The little guy on the screen had moved. He was in there jumping around and kicking his legs – miniscule though they were!

I really could hardly believe it. After months of grief, days filled with the silence of the empty crib, and nights of heart wrenching tears, my baby was really and truly going to make it.

It was finally time to dream. And dream I did.

◊ ◊ ◊

That sweet baby was born seven months later weighing 9 lbs. 3 ozs. A boy that blessed our lives so immensely! Loving him, training him, we never forgot those who went before him.

Over the time when we were celebrating his first birthday, I once again found myself with a test showing two pink lines. Feeling much more confident, I began applying natural progesterone cream to help my body sustain this pregnancy.

Yet fear is hard to root out when it's been in your heart a long time. Only this fear became a reality. We lost that precious baby at 5 ½ weeks. Less than two weeks after I had found out it was on the way.

Once again the grief, doubt, and questions overwhelmed me. Was this going to be a struggle my entire fertile years? Would I never be able to enjoy a pregnancy just as a simple pregnancy?

Many books and articles will tell you that you are more fertile immediately following a miscarriage. And since this miscarriage was so incredibly early, and seemed more like a really heavy period, we decided to keep trying.

One month later, I again held a positive pregnancy test in my hand. I was becoming a pro at spotting the two pink lines that form when a new little one is on the way!

And just like the previous healthy pregnancy, this one had a distinct feeling about it. **It had the feeling of life that would not go away!** I have no idea if those two healthy babies had implanted strong enough that it triggered more hormone production. I really don't know since I don't understand all the science behind it. All I knew was that this baby felt as though it was going to make it too.

Eight months later, he was born within four hours of labor in the midst of the storm of the decade. The hospital basement had flooded due to the amount of rain in the previous twelve hours, so we climbed all the flights of stairs required to reach the maternity ward.

With barely enough time for the doctor to pull his gloves on, the little guy made his entrance to this big, bright world! He was here. He was alive. And he was just as precious as those gone before him.

◊ ◊ ◊

Life became busy with two small children, as you moms will know! When the second little guy had reached eight months, I found to my surprise that I was pregnant again.

This was truly a surprise, but losing babies has a unique way of making you love each and every baby that comes – planned or not.

Just like the other pregnancies, it was a wait-and-see. However, it went by with no serious mishaps and a sweet baby girl was born eight months later!

By this time, I had a pretty good handle on my low progesterone and no longer supplemented with it. We went on to have two more healthy pregnancies, resulting in five sweet children here on earth with us.

◊ ◊ ◊

Many years passed.

Then almost twelve years from the time I first saw two pink lines with my very first baby, I once again held a test showing that another little one was on the way.

Time had been good to me in that it had blurred many of the memories surrounding my earlier miscarriages. I had grown confident in my body to sustain pregnancies, and had said hello to four precious, squirming darlings since those heart-shattering days.

Then life took me down a path I never thought I'd have to walk again.

I started bleeding.

In shock, I watched as time replayed itself out before my eyes. The spotting. Then the bleeding. And the tests that came back confirming what I knew in my heart. My baby had gone Home.

I felt like someone had taken the film of my life and pushed rewind. Making me relive every single painful moment. Why was I being asked to do this yet again? Hadn't I given enough babies to grace Heaven's golden streets that I should be allowed to keep this one?

Anger and grief tore my heart wide open as I struggled with accepting this. I struggled with my God.

A God who was so faithful to me during my times of grief and confusion. A God who lovingly waited until I could bow my head and say "Not my will, but Thine be done."

Even though my heart was shattering in the silence of the nursery, my grief may have overwhelmed me as I looked at the stillness of the rocking chair, and the tears that flowed all night long – my God was still with me. He had a purpose, and He had a plan.

And I chose to trust that plan. *Although I had no idea what it was.*

That precious little baby took a long time for me to get over. I had had so many hopes and dreams that had come crashing down to lay in rubble at my feet.

It took time for my heart to trust again. To learn to laugh again. To wake up and say "Maybe life will be good again."

Several months later, I found out I was pregnant for the tenth time in my life. This time I again went the natural supplement route, especially considering I now had a midwife, and began using progesterone cream. I also used an herbal supplement that had been formulated specifically for threatened pregnancies.

The bleeding slowed and stopped. I went in to take some blood tests. But as I waited on the test results to come back, I began to get sick. Morning sickness was hitting early this time.

When the test results came back showing the baby still alive, I knew we were going to make it. This sweet little baby was really going to be born!

Morning sickness was the worst it had ever been. And if you read much on miscarriages, you will know that morning sickness is actually a good sign of a healthy pregnancy. Yet when you are in the midst of it, it is hard to be thankful for it.

Eight months later, healthy baby number six was born at home to much love and anticipation!

My heart bowed before an Almighty God who has the power to give life, to take it, and to see my faith through the grief of losing those four sweet babies. Faith that grew stronger because it drove me to the Rock of Ages.

"And said, Naked came I out of my mother's womb, and naked shall I return thither: the LORD gave, and the LORD hath taken away; blessed be the name of the LORD."

Job 1:21

Life As God Sees It: The Biblical Principle of Life Within the Womb

I would wait until my husband was out the door for work, and then I would cry. And cry. And cry. Dark days were nothing new as I floundered in my pit of grief, not knowing how to help myself up and over the side to solid ground once again.

There had been no preparation for what I was dealing with. I was lost in a sea of depression, tears and confusion. How would I ever find my way out?

But God was faithful and He began to show me some beautiful, Biblical truths regarding life from conception. And how to deal with death in the womb.

◊ ◊ ◊

God loves life.

God Himself is the Giver of Life, the Creator of all mankind, the One who breathed the breath of life into us.

This is the Biblical principle upon which this book is founded, and upon which we base all assumptions of conception and the value of a soul.

It is this principle that will lift you up out of your well of silent grief. It is this principle that will let you grieve silently no longer.

But what does God actually say about it? From where are we basing this assumption that God loves life? Come walk with me on a beautiful pathway through the Scriptures as we take a quick look at what God truly says about it.

*"And the Lord God formed man of the dust of the ground, and **breathed into his nostrils the breath of life**, and man became a living soul." Genesis 2:7*

*"For Thou hast possessed my reins: **Thou hast covered me in my mother's womb**. I will praise Thee; for I am fearfully and wonderfully made: marvelous are Thy works; and that my soul knoweth right well. My substance was not hid from Thee, when I was made in secret, and curiously wrought in the lowest parts of the earth. Thine eyes did see my substance, yet being unperfect; and in thy book all my members were written, which in continuance were fashioned, when as yet there was none of them." Psalm 139:13-16*

*"**Before I formed thee in the belly I knew thee**; and before thou camest forth out of the womb I sanctified thee, and I ordained thee a prophet unto the nations." Jeremiah 1:5*

*"Lo, children are an heritage of the Lord: and **the fruit of the womb is His reward**." Psalm 127:3*

*"Thus saith the Lord, thy Redeemer, and **He that formed thee from the womb**, I*

am the Lord that maketh all things; that stretcheth froth the heavens alone; that spreadeth abroad the earth by myself."
Isaiah 44:24

"Listen, O isles, unto me; and hearken, ye people, from far; The Lord hath called me from the womb; ***from the bowels of my mother hath He made mention of my name."*** *Isaiah 49:1*

"But Jesus said, Suffer little children, and forbid them not, to come unto Me: for of such is the kingdom of heaven." *Matthew 19:14*

◊ ◊ ◊

When I was in the midst of my grief with my very first miscarriage, I realized how taboo of a subject miscarriage was at that time. Especially when the miscarriage is an early one with no "baby" to show for it. There is no memorial service, no grave, no headstone. No sympathy cards that come rushing in the mail.

This has changed somewhat in the years since my first miscarriage, but back then it seemed an almost dirty subject to discuss anything pregnancy-related for the first three months of the baby's life in utero. I never understood this. I was always overjoyed to find myself pregnant and couldn't imagine why anyone would want to wait twelve whole weeks to tell anybody. Yeah, I was one of those annoying ones who had to bite my tongue to keep it quiet for just two weeks!

However, I finally caught on that those who waited three months to tell anyone about a pregnancy did so because of the possibility of miscarriage. And this is a completely personal choice, but I will tell you my experience with this choice.

With some of my pregnancies, I told right away. Others I waited a few weeks. With some of the miscarriages, very few people had even known I was pregnant.

I soon discovered that folks found out when you lost a baby – even if you had never told them you were pregnant to begin with. For some reason that information seems to fly pretty fast. So I was finding myself receiving condolences, even though I had purposely told few people about the pregnancy. This shows I was surrounded by people who loved and cared for me. People who hurt when I was hurting.

But it also cleared up one thing for me: since folks found out when I lost a baby anyway, why not let them in on the joy when I found out I was expecting one? So from then on, I usually shared the happy news within a week or two of finding out.

It also helped solidify in my mind the Biblical truth that was becoming clearer all the time. My baby was a precious soul with an eternal future. **It deserved joy at its coming . . . and grief at its leaving.**

This was extremely important in how I dealt with my miscarriages. I began to view my baby through God's eyes. He had a purpose in putting it here for a few weeks. He had a purpose in taking it Home so soon. He knew what He was doing because He had lovingly formed that precious child within me.

If God loved this child so much . . . I would love it too. And in the loving, I would open my heart to not only the joy that came with knowing it was on the way, but also to the deep pain that came when it was taken away.

This truth left me free to grieve this sweet baby like it deserved to be grieved by a mother who would lay down her life for her child.

Babies are so infinitely precious, whether seen or unseen. When you begin to view life through the eyes of God, it gives you the license to cry all night long. For you are commemorating the short life of your own flesh and blood - before they were called Home.

It is okay to be sad. It's normal to be depressed for days. You are not crazy if you cry for hours on end for a sweet baby that weighed only a few ounces.

◊ ◊ ◊

<u>If there is one truth I want you to take away
from this book, it is this:</u>

**From the moment God breathed life into
your baby,**

**He also gave you the right to mourn the
death of that same baby.**

From The Depths of Grief

While struggling through my miscarriages, I found that writing down my thoughts and feelings provided healing for my broken heart. I would encourage any mother who is dealing with a miscarriage to do the same. Not only does it give you a place to question, to cry, and to commemorate, but you will be amazed at how the memories fade ten years down the road. Keeping a journal or diary let me remember the precious children that I never knew.

It let me remember long after the tears had dried, the pain had subsided, and the dark days had ended. For myself, I find it strengthens my faith in God to read back through my writings and realize how far He has brought me on the path to healing.

I am going to share with you some of those writings that came out of the depths of my grief. And pray you will be blessed by them.

◊ ◊ ◊

Sent To Heaven With Love

From the first moment I knew you were there, I also knew you might not be with us for very long. Icy fear gripped my heart as I held my breath and waited.

I did not want to love . . . . . . only to lose yet again. I knew how much that hurts.

But then I heard a sweet whisper —

"Why can you not love me just for me?"

And slowly the fear that clutched my heart began to loosen its strangle hold. For I realized how selfish it was to withhold my love from my own flesh and blood, no matter how deep the pain it might inflict on my own heart.

My dreams for you were not big ones. They did not reach farther than this moment in time. But nonetheless, they were hopes and dreams of you, my precious baby. Each moment I carried you was bittersweet, knowing it was only for a little while. Yet the memories of these few short weeks, I will carry in my heart forever.

I do not understand why God must have one more child to fill the portals of Heaven.

I wish I could see this heartbreak through His eyes.

Yet for some reason, God has need of you there. Perhaps it is to watch over the three who have gone before you.

And so, my precious darling . . . . I send you to Heaven with love. Go Home, sweet Baby, and wait for me there.

◊ ◊ ◊

Sweet Babies, You're Gone

Sweet babies, you're gone — oh what shall I

do?

Shall I mourn, shall I weep, shall I cry out

for you?

My aching arms long to cuddle you close,

To count your fingers and kiss your pink

nose.

Someday up in Heaven, my sweet ones, we'll

meet.

And here's what we'll do at our dear Savior's

feet —

We'll laugh and we'll giggle and hold hands
all day.

Then I'll whisper the words I've been
longing to say:

"My darlings, I love you."

The Day That Never Was

I knew this day was coming. I'd had eight months to prepare for it. But still it stared me in the face, taunting me with what "could have been".

It was the due date of my pregnancy that ended in a miscarriage.

Eight months before, I had said good-bye to a sweet baby that I never really knew – yet had loved anyway. How was I do deal with this day? It felt as though I had begun to get over the miscarriage, only to have the due date to hurdle myself over too.

With my last miscarriage, I found myself writing down my feelings. It was a release for me, a letting-go of all the "what ifs" and moving on to the future and the eternal hope of heaven. Heaven that now held four of the sweetest blessings to ever grace my life.

Yet I needed one more day to say good-bye.

◇ ◇ ◇

The Day That Never Was

This was the day that should have been.

But it isn't.

Many think I should be okay with this day.

But I'm not.

For this was the day I should have held you in my arms. I would have labored for hours, endured horrible pain, and then finally heard your sweet newborn cry.

All I hear is my heart shattering in the silence.

There should be size 1 diapers on the changing table and freshly-washed sleepers in the drawer. Baby powder on the shelf and tiny socks in the basket.

Only God knows how I cannot look at the places where all these things should have been.

I thought I'd be tough enough to stand against all the emotions this day would hold. Be the kind of woman who has strength and grace in the midst of sadness.

What a traitor the human heart is . . . **I'm praying tomorrow holds strength.**

I was counting on the day when I would swaddle you in a fuzzy blanket, hold you close, and breathe in your fresh, newborn smell.

Those blankets are still tucked away.

I would have proudly shown you to all my friends for the beautiful baby you were.

Instead, all I feel is a tightness around my heart as I think of what could have been.

We were going to be a little team — you and I. Rocking together in our rocking chair. Snuggled up with blankets and pillows.

The rocking chair still rocks. **But it's missing a sweet, vital part of it — you.**

You would have depended upon me every minute of every hour those first few months. For feeding, bathing, dressing, sleeping, and loving.

The seconds tick by so slowly today. Will tomorrow never come?

I knew this day was coming. This day that should have been.

And again my heart is breaking for the precious darling that took wings and flew too soon to Heaven.

Yet while I mourn the day that never came, my heart lives for the day that of a certainty will be.

The day I get to see you running through the fields of Heaven will finally be the time when my heart can rest.

For there will never come another day that never was.

(written and posted on our blog, Living in the Shoe)

For those of you who are dealing with the due date of your miscarriage, remember that once again - **it is okay to cry.** I found that more healing took place once I got on the other side of the due date. So keep hope, you will find yourself smiling once again. You will wake up one day and realize that the sun is shining and you feel like taking another small step to embracing life and hope.

Cling to the hand of the God who made you and your precious baby, the One who loved you enough to die for you, and the Healer who promises to one day wipe away all tears.

The Practical Side of Miscarriage

This chapter might tend to be a little gory, so if you are at all squeamish, please be forewarned! When presented with the idea of a threatening miscarriage, I began to search the internet. How would this take place? What exactly was happening to my body? Would it hurt badly? Could I hemorrhage?

Frankly, I was scared.

Now let me preface this all by saying that every woman's experience will be different. Miscarriages can vary in their intensity with the length of the pregnancy, a woman's unique pain threshold and even complications. In fact, if you are a multiple miscarriage survivor like I am, you may find each miscarriage is different from the previous ones. So please keep this in mind while reading through this chapter.

What are the symptoms of an early miscarriage?

Like I mentioned above, each woman's miscarriage will be different but if you have any of these symptoms within the first few weeks, please call your doctor immediately.

- Bleeding or spotting – This is the telltale sign of miscarriage, but it doesn't always mean you are going to lose your baby. I've had at least two pregnancies with spotting and bleeding, and still went on to keep the baby. But it definitely warrants a call to the doctor. If your bleeding becomes excessive or bright red blood and gushing – go to an emergency room immediately! Hemorrhaging can happen and is not something to waste any time with.
- Severe cramping
- Back ache
- Unexplained fever
- Abdominal pain
- Weakness

- Sudden decrease in morning sickness or pregnancy symptoms

What will my doctor do with a threatened miscarriage?

If this is the first time you have shown symptoms of a threatening miscarriage, your doctor will probably tell you to rest and drink plenty of water. Get off your feet, woman and take it easy!

Now the jury is still out on whether or not this will prevent a miscarriage, but it will at least take some of the stress off of your body. Miscarriages are caused by different things and at this point, you don't know if yours is one that could be helped by bedrest or not – so be safe and lay down.

He will probably see what your spotting or cramping does for the next 24 hours as to what he does next. If your spotting turns into full-out bleeding, you will most likely be checking yourself into the ultrasound room pretty quickly.

Ultrasounds are not always the first thing they will do, but it is the easiest way to detect a heartbeat from about 7-10 weeks. This is after the baby is big enough to be seen via ultrasound, and yet it's still too small for a heartbeat to be detected by Doppler.

It's possible your doctor will also order you some lab work. He is checking your HCG levels. HCG stands for Human Chorionic Gonadotropin. This is the precious little hormone given off by a portion of the placenta once your baby has implanted into the lining of your uterus. It is what caused those two pink lines to appear on your positive pregnancy test!

Your doctor is checking to see if your HCG levels rise accordingly. He most likely will order a quantitative HCG blood test – this doesn't just check to see if you have the HCG hormone present, but at what level it currently is at. If you are a pregnancy nut like me, you will be highly interested in this test. It tells you if your pregnancy is viable or not.

The HCG level usually doubles every 48-72 hours, depending on what week you are at in your pregnancy. However, this is approximate, but gives a rough guideline for the doctors to follow. If the level is rising, but slowly, there is still a chance of the pregnancy making it. However, if your levels have fallen, it means Jesus took your sweet one Home to be with Him.

Will it hurt?

This answer will be unique to each woman's pain threshold and to the length of her pregnancy. I found that my very early miscarriages, the ones that happened at 5-6 weeks, were really not much more than a hard and painful period.

But my first miscarriage was a strange one – which goes to show you that each one may be different. I bled quite a bit when it occurred in May, passed the baby, the sack and placenta – but it wasn't anything horribly traumatizing. Throughout the summer, I had several normal periods. In August, I had a horrible, horrible period with such severe cramping I probably should have called my doctor. The cramping culminated in me passing some strange, gray tissue. And, no, I was not pregnant. After my miscarriage, I had been taking some hormone-regulating herbal supplements and I wonder if it wasn't helping my body get rid of some old tissue from my miscarriage. Whatever it was, it grossed me out!

Some women with babies that died in the 9-13 week range find they might actually be experiencing a mini-birth. Their baby has formed enough and is big enough that it takes actual contractions for the uterus to open up so the baby can be expelled.

So, yes. Miscarriage can hurt. But it can also be not much more than a heavy period.

My advice to you is this: whether your miscarriage is very early or late enough for actual contractions – **please do not be alone!** There is the possibility of hemorrhaging and you need someone there to support you and call the doctor if needed. If you are travelling and begin a miscarriage with moderate to heavy bleeding – in other words, you **know** this miscarriage is going to happen and happen now – I would stop at a motel with a hospital close by. Just don't take chances.

What do I do with the baby's remains?

This is the hard question. And one that will vary with different women, the development of the baby and your circumstances.

Some women find they will do one of these:

- Bury the baby someplace special
- Give the baby to the doctor for testing (your doctor may actually require this)
- Just let it go with the rest of the pregnancy remains – especially if the baby is not recognizable from the placenta and sack (sometimes it has all deteriorated to where you cannot

distinguish one part of the uterine contents from another)

- Give the baby to someone else and let them decide – I did this with my first pregnancy. I gave the baby's remains to my mother and told her to do something with it. I honestly don't remember if I ever found out what she did with my baby. But I knew that she loved me and I couldn't emotionally handle taking care of it myself.

How do I commemorate my baby?

There are several ways to remember this precious child and some women like to do something special. However, you will find each woman grieves differently and therefore, some women wish to get over it and on with their lives and healthier pregnancies. Neither way is wrong. We all deal with grief in our own unique ways. You need to do what helps you heal from the pain of losing your baby!

Some women like to plant a tree or a rose bush in commemoration of their baby. I know my mother-in-law purchased Gideon Bibles for others in remembrance of my miscarried babies.

Another way some women remember their baby is by doing something special on their miscarried baby's due date. You could have a small party, commemorating the life that still lives – just not on earth with us!

Whatever you do, let it be something special – for your baby was special.

How long must I wait before trying to get pregnant again?

Your doctor will probably give you the general rule-of-thumb that all medical personnel give: wait three months for your body to heal before trying.

There is much sense in this guideline. Your body has gone through severe stress and it is possible you might even have such complications as low iron levels from abnormal bleeding. They give this guideline to give you time to build your blood levels back up, regain your strength and also to help you heal emotionally.

Now not all women will follow this guideline. I didn't. But I also never had a "later" early miscarriage. My latest was at nine weeks, with the others being much earlier – so most of mine were more like heavy periods. I never got extremely iron-deficient from them or had complications.

It is also said that some women are more fertile immediately following a miscarriage. This, too, was factored into our decision to try immediately with most of our miscarriages.

However, I am not a doctor so please ask your doctor for his opinion.

How do I deal with a pregnancy following a miscarriage?

Lots of trust in God Almighty.

A pregnancy following a miscarriage can be a very fearful time. Every time you go to the bathroom, you'll be checking for spotting. Every time your stomach feels good and not nauseous, you will panic and think your morning sickness has abruptly left. Every time you start cramping, you'll find yourself on Google – and scared.

You might also feel cheated. Cheated because your miscarriage has now taken the joy out of pregnancy that most women feel. This is normal for us survivors of miscarriage.

I honestly have no magic ticket for getting through the pregnancy scares, but simply taking it one day at a time. I know it felt like I was holding my breath through the first twelve weeks of pregnancy – until I could say that I'd finally reached the "safe stage". It always helped to get past the week where I'd lost my previous baby.

One thing your doctor might be willing to do is an ultrasound to set your mind at ease. Now I will tell you to do your own research regarding ultrasounds and the safety of multiple ones, but with my last miscarriage, I was such a scared mess that I scheduled an ultrasound around 8 weeks. And we found a baby with a heartbeat! This did so much for setting my mind at ease.

You could also request to have your HCG levels drawn to see what they are doing – going up or down and how fast they are rising.

And remember: **you are not in this alone**. God is right there to walk alongside you in this fearful time of your pregnancy.

Their Stories

I couldn't hold back the tears as I typed this chapter. These special women have given me their stories to share with you and I am so glad they were willing to open their hearts and allow us a glimpse into their pain – and how they dealt with it!

◊ ◊ ◊

Loss at 12 Weeks

First I must say that I have had several early miscarriages which led us to use a low dose fertility drug, clomid. I was 22 when I got married and felt I was born to be a wife and mother. Those were actually the only two jobs I wished to be blessed with. Since I was able to obtain the "job" of being a wife, becoming a mother should've come next right? But it didn't come easy. I had several miscarriages and through testing the doctors suggested using a low dose fertility drug, clomid. I was very eager while my husband was more skeptical.

Within 3 months we were pregnant and were elated. Within 3 more months we lost our first baby at 12 weeks. I was showing and wearing maternity clothes so it was well known we were expecting. The baby died and it took two weeks before I fully miscarried. My doctor wanted to do a procedure called a DNC and I wouldn't allow it. I specifically said that if my baby was going to be with God it would be God's work to take him or her. I went through actual labor at home and delivered a "blob". The experience totally scared my husband and he was not as quick as I was to want to try again. He was more worried about me and my health, physically and emotionally.

The only way I made it through was through the grace of God and my husband. All that kept me going to try again was thinking "the Lord blessed me once and showed me all things are possible through him."

After that miscarriage we used the low dose fertility drugs and had 2 sons two years apart. Five years later we tried again for one last time with the same fertility drugs and we lost that pregnancy at 7 weeks. I was devastated because I knew that was our last chance since, as a couple, we had decided the Lord blessed us with two sons and we were so thankful that we were not going to try again.

One night I was giving my 2nd son a bath and he was almost 4 1/2 years old, he said, "Mommy, you are going to have a baby and it's gonna be a girl and her name's gonna be Hannah." Well my boys were young and had no idea we had just suffered a miscarriage and I cried and cried and just told him how much I loved having him and his brother and how lucky we all are to spend so much time together and we weren't going to think about adding any more babies to our perfect family. But he insisted I was to have another baby and soon.

Little did I know he was right! I thought I was dying of something because I was so sick and lost almost 10 pounds and soon found out I was absolutely expecting. I couldn't believe it! The Lord absolutely blessed us with an amazing miracle in giving us another son! I am now wife, mom to 3 sons, 19, 16 and 11, mother in law and memaw to one granddaughter and anxiously awaiting the birth of my first grandson. God is good!

~ Melissa Cummins

◊ ◊ ◊

Loss at 8 Weeks

After 3 perfect, healthy pregnancies, deliveries, and babies in 4 years, a positive pregnancy test was...normal. I found myself on a Sunday morning sitting in the bathroom staring blankly at a "positive". I wish I could say that my initial reaction was "Thank you Lord!" But truthfully, it was more of a "Really Lord!?! Are you sure this is what you want for us?" (I confess that I was tired of being pregnant and overwhelmed with three kids 3 and under)

My husband reacted the same, but after talking it over for a few moments we laughed, threw our hands in the air and said, "OK! 4 IT IS!!!!" The next few weeks flew by without much notice. I did comment to my husband at one point that things didn't feel right. I was supposed to be 7 weeks, which usually is the turning point for me, but I felt fine. He brushed it off as no big deal, however; a week later on June 6th 2013 I started spotting.

That was not normal for me. I called my husband home, we found someone to watch our kids and headed to the ER. We rode in silence. I knew in my heart that we were losing our baby. After bloodwork and an ultrasound it was confirmed, baby #4, the baby we had been tossing names around for just a few days earlier - was in Glory and we were in pieces. We prayed on the ride home, thanking God for loving us, for loving our baby, and we stood on what we knew about Him, that He is good!

Telling everyone was hard. Standing up in the same church that just 4 short weeks earlier my husband had announced our pregnancy in was harder. All I could say through the tears was Job 1:21 "The Lord gives, and the Lord takes away, Blessed be the name of the Lord."

Life went on. Three little children awoke every morning needing mommy to provide for them and take care of them and love them. I was a pillar of strength during the day and a mess of tears and pain once the last little eye closed and I collapsed into my husband's arms. I searched my Bible for every verse I could find on comfort, strength, God's love...one stuck out to me and I clung to it with everything I had. "From the end of the earth I call to You when my heart is faint; Lead me to the rock that is higher than I." Psalm 61:2.

My heart was so faint...it was broken. And the only way I could go through my day was to lean on the One who was stronger and higher than me.

I found myself 6 weeks post-loss again sitting in the bathroom staring at another positive pregnancy test. My first thought..."Not again", immediately followed by a peace that passes all understanding. I knew in my spirit that this baby would make it. My OB didn't believe I could possibly be pregnant and ordered an ultrasound to see. Sure enough...there was a baby, heartbeat and all.

We conceived 10 days after losing baby #4! It wasn't an easy pregnancy emotionally. I didn't know how to mourn a loss and celebrate new life at the same time, but the Lord walked me through each day and I learned that accepting our loss, grieving it deeply and enjoying every sign of life from the new baby could be done simultaneously. I cried a lot, thought about our baby in heaven and the loss of their future with us on earth while daydreaming about holding my baby girl.

In March of 2014 we welcomed Harmony Ruth into our family. God is good! It is a regular part of life in this house to talk about the miscarriage. My 3 year old daughter (who was 2 at the time) asks me almost weekly questions about "the baby that died in my belly". In a way it keeps the baby alive to us, his/her death is a part of all of us and has opened the door multiple times for us to share the gospel with our children as we talk about death and eternal life.

There was a purpose for that life, even though it was brief and quiet. Lessons were learned, faith was stretched, time with our children is now appreciated a little bit more. And we have someone very special waiting to hug our necks when we are called home!

~ Lacey

◊ ◊ ◊

Loss at 10 Weeks

I will tell you about my first of 5 miscarriages as that one was the most traumatic. It was a little over 22 years ago when I found out that I was pregnant again. We were really excited even though our little girl was only 8 months old. Everything had gone perfectly fine for my first pregnancy so I never ever gave it a thought that something like a miscarriage could happen to me. They just happened to other people, right? I didn't get sick but I figured that would be coming as I was dreadfully sick with my first pregnancy. At 10 weeks I started to bleed and went to see the doctor. He could not get a heartbeat and said that I was headed for a miscarriage. I thought that maybe if I took it easy it would be ok but he was sure that that would not be the case. He assured me that since we did not have any insurance I would be just fine passing it at home. Had he not told me that, I would have definitely gone to the hospital as it was not a pleasant experience.

Afterward I became a bit depressed as I wondered "Why Me?" My other friends were having babies and had no trouble. One thing that sticks out to me as an encouragement was an older lady at church wrote me letter and told me that years before she had gone through the same thing and she feels for me. Now I try to do the same when I know of someone that has just had a miscarriage.

With all my miscarriages I usually later could see that God knew best. After my first miscarriage we had the opportunity to go to Japan and the Philippines. Had I been pregnant we could not have gone as it would have been close to my due date.

There are a few things you should never say to someone who has just gone through a miscarriage. "Why don't you just get over it?" or "What's the big deal, you can have another baby", or "Maybe you should just be happy with your 2 girls and 2 boys and not try for another baby".

The experience of going through a miscarriage taught me to be more thankful for the child or children we had. It also reminded me every time I was pregnant to be thankful for being sick, since if I was not sick then the pregnancy would end in a miscarriage. It also helped me to be more sympathetic to others when they go through the same experience.

~ Michelle

◊ ◊ ◊

Loss at 5-6 Weeks

I have had quite a few miscarriages that ended in the very early stages. I would miss my period, and get sick right away - and yes, that has always been me. And then a few days or up to 2 wks later I would lose my dear little one!

I had 2 C-sections, 1 still born, and another c- section. So I had lots of scar tissue. Did you know that every time you are expecting a new little one, it attaches at a different place in your uterus? I was able to get pregnant but wasn't able to carry the little one. It was heart breaking, my sister in laws and cousins were having little ones, and oh how my mommy heart longed for a sweet little bundle to hold.

I would have about 2 weeks of extreme hormonal swings, then my period. And then only to start it all over again. I can hear you say now why didn't you give your body a chance to heal? Well, we wanted a little one so badly that we kept trying.

Finally we laid our desires down, and pursued adoption. After our son was born for us, and he was 3 months old, God blessed with a miracle baby! All went well. We are very thankful for our miracle son, and I think often of my dear little ones who are in heaven!

~ Tina Zimmerman

◊ ◊ ◊

Loss at 6 Weeks

We got married in June of 2000. Our first son arrived in August of 2001, and our second son in December of 2003. In spite of the fact that I'd always had an oddly long cycle, I got pregnant without even trying and had easy-breezy pregnancies. After our second son was born, we began hoping for a girl to soon join our family.

But it wasn't until the early summer of 2006 that I conceived again. We were ecstatic---until I started spotting at around 6 weeks. I made an appointment with my OB/GYN immediately. My old doctor had retired, and I saw the new, much younger doctor. After performing an internal exam, he congratulated us, waved aside our concern about the bleeding episode, and told me that I was about 7 weeks pregnant. Relieved, we called our families and began spreading the news even though it was early in the pregnancy. We also decided that we did not like the new doctor at all, so I switched to a Certified Nurse Midwife & made an appointment for 2 weeks later.

I'll never forget walking into her office that beautiful summer day. My life felt so perfect, so blessed. Within an hour or two, however, my world had fallen apart. The first red flag was when the midwife's standard pregnancy test read negative. She asked about the earlier bleeding, and consulted with the doctor who had examined me. Then she sent us for an ultrasound (something the doctor had not done).

Having been through several ultrasounds with my first two pregnancies, I knew almost as soon as the technician did that something was horribly wrong. Where there should have been a tiny bundle of activity and a rapidly-beating heart "blink", there was an empty black hole. The young technician cried as she told us what we already knew: there was no baby. I remember my husband holding me close and asking me, "Can you still love God?" And my numb reply, "I don't know."

Later, our midwife told us that our baby had likely been gone for a week before the doctor had examined me, and that he had made a grave mistake in telling me that all was fine. It took me a long time to forgive him for giving us that false hope, and I never went to his office again.

Sadly, this was only the beginning of our journey, and it was also the beginning of my journey into depression. For the following year, we tried to get pregnant with no success. Then in the early summer of 2007, the home pregnancy test gave a positive result, and we rejoiced. But again, at 6 weeks, I started bleeding. This time, there was no false hope, no excited announcements, no need for the ultrasound, because we knew what was happening. Almost exactly a year after my first miscarriage, I was having another one. This time, I was much more aware of what was taking place, and I was able to bury what I believed was an oh-so-tiny baby.

My heart said that it was a girl, although of course there was no way to tell for sure. This time, we chose a name: Destiny Hope. Destiny means "a predetermined course of events considered as something beyond human power or control" and Hope means "a feeling of expectation and desire for a certain thing to happen; a feeling of trust."

A few months later, I experienced what we were certain was a third miscarriage, although we never had it verified by a doctor. We knew the signs all too well. Christmas of 2007 was a terribly low time for me, spiritually and emotionally. So I felt like I'd been punched in the gut when my brother and his wife announced their pregnancy at our family Christmas dinner. I spent the rest of the weekend in an aching haze of hurt as I longed for the baby who "should" have been due in two months' time.

Little did I realize that a miracle was already unfolding in my womb. A few weeks later, I was at the doctor for a series of tests, since we had decided to try to find out the reasons for my wacky hormonal cycles, the infertility/pregnancy loss, and the continued depression. A couple of days later, the nurse called to give me some results, and she asked if I was sitting down. Then she said the words I'll never forget, "Honey, you're pregnant!! And you're about 12 weeks along!"

The realization that we were already way past that dreaded 6-week mark was a gift from God, and an incredible relief. That pregnancy was a very difficult one for me, the complete opposite of my first two. Then we nearly lost our daughter in childbirth, so she is our miracle baby twice over. Her birth marked the beginning of my healing process, and more than 6 years later, I still feel so overwhelmed with gratitude that God gave her to us. Her name simply means "holy" and "pure." A miracle.

Four years later, we were beginning to accept that our family was finished, when God surprised us with a little boy. It was another long, difficult pregnancy, but his name carries the meaning of being a gift from God that is given back to Him to bring to fulfillment (or to close) a vow. It also means to draw near to God. As long and painful as my journey through pregnancy loss, secondary infertility, and depression has been, I am also just beginning to see the beauty of it all. I now realize that the question is not so much, "Can I still love God?" as it is, "Does God still love me?" The resounding, amazing answer is, "Yes. Always. No matter the pain, no matter the hurt, no matter the depths of my grief, He loves me." And that is enough.

~ Joanna Yoder

◊ ◊ ◊

Loss at 5-6 Weeks

I found out that we were expecting our 5th baby at the end of October, 2014. I was excited! My kids and husband were as well. As usual, we announced the news of a new blessing to our friends and family very quickly. I knit a baby hat and used that in our photo announcement.

Unfortunately, I woke up to discover that I was spotting only 5.5 weeks into the pregnancy. It was a Thursday. I took it easy for the day and the bleeding got a bit heavier. I tried to hold on to hope that the baby was still OK. My husband came home early from work and I went to get bloodwork done to check the pregnancy hormone levels in my blood. I passed a noticeable clot the next morning but bleeding subsided quite a bit. My husband more or less ordered me to do nothing all weekend.

We had to wait until Monday to get a second vial of blood taken so that the hormone levels could be compared. We found out on the Tuesday that we had indeed lost our baby. I believe that a baby is a life from the start. I found myself almost wishing that I didn't hold these beliefs. I know it's not true, but I couldn't help but wonder if it wouldn't be easier to accept a miscarriage this early if I thought the baby wasn't a baby yet. I felt like I was over-reacting. After all, we had only known about the pregnancy for barely 2 weeks.

I also had a good friend who discovered she had lost her baby the same weekend. The difference was, this was her 4th loss in a year and she was in the second trimester. I felt like my loss was so much less significant than hers. We spent the next weeks in a lot of prayer for each other and my friend assured me, through her own grief, that my grief was real and valid - normal as well.

I am thankful that my miscarriage was physically uncomplicated. I had to trust that God had a purpose for this. I'm not sure what it is, but my baby's whole purpose in life was accomplished in only a few weeks' time. I choose to believe this because it's too hard to think that a baby could die for no reason at all; that that precious life had no meaning or purpose.

~ Savannah Berniquez

◊ ◊ ◊

Loss at 6, 4 and 4 Weeks

In April of 2014 I had the first miscarriage I had ever had in my life. After having two amazing pregnancies, I never thought it would happen to me. I started bleeding the day before I was supposed to go to my first prenatal appointment. I truly felt like someone had hit me in my chest when the doctor told me I was miscarrying. I was told the statistic, 1 out of every 4 women's pregnancies will end in a loss, but still felt like I had done something wrong. The doctor told me to wait two cycles and then to try again if my husband and I were ready.

On June 15th, I had my second miscarriage. I didn't make an appointment this time because I knew what was going on and didn't feel like hearing the doctor tell me the statistics yet again.

After that miscarriage, I found out that I was pregnant again. I lost that pregnancy July 15th. I didn't have any prenatal care or anything - I was just told to go to the emergency room.

Three weeks later I found I was yet again pregnant. This time my husband and I didn't try. We had started natural family planning and had wanted to try again next year. We thought that my body just needed some time. I didn't have any excitement whatsoever. I was terribly upset, mad, scared, and in disbelief. I wasn't ready to go through another miscarriage mentally or physically.

This time I did make an appointment but with a high risk doctor just in case there was something they could do to save my pregnancy. My pregnancy started out terrible. I had an ultrasound to see how far along I was. I was 4 weeks and 4 days and there in my uterus was a little gestational sac but it was surrounded by some kind of fluid. The doctors told me before I left the doctor's office that if I had any bleeding, to call them or go to my local emergency room.

They scheduled me for another ultrasound. This time the gestational sac was twice as big but the High Risk Fetal Developmental Specialist who looked at the sonogram told the doctor that he wasn't sure if he could see anything. I was told again that it wasn't certain if I would keep this pregnancy and that if I had any bleeding to call or go to my local E.R.

I was scheduled for another ultrasound, this time it would be in two weeks. Let me tell you, it was the longest two weeks of my life. The day of my ultrasound I cried and was extremely nervous. When the doctor put the probe on my tummy and to my disbelief - there sat my new little baby! Strong heartbeat and everything.

I even got to see the baby move a little. It truly was the most amazing thing I had ever seen in the past few years after my daughters were born. Today I am 26 weeks and 1 day with a little boy. My husband and I have decided that since we have two beautiful daughters and soon to be handsome son, we will be done with having children. Our family is finally complete!

~ Racheal Heath

◊ ◊ ◊

Loss at 12 Weeks

My husband and I had been thinking of trying to have another baby because our youngest was reaching the 9mo mark. We started talking about it and praying about it, but since I was still breastfeeding we didn't really think about it much. It wasn't long afterwards that we were celebrating our youngest's first birthday and thoughts of having another baby were festering in the backs of our minds. I went in for my yearly exam and was surprised to find out that we were expecting our 4th baby and the baby was quite established. We were excited, praising God and even the oldest 2 children were excited and praying for a brother to add to our mix. I began spotting the day AFTER finding out we were expecting our 4th blessing and I just knew.

My husband put me on bed rest "just in case" and within 24 hours, our wonderful blessing was ushered into the arms of Jesus. Unexplainable heartbreak, depression and worst of all ANGER. I was angry with God for allowing me to find out one day and lose him/her the very next. I was hurt and I didn't understand WHY. My heart broke each time my little girls asked me where the baby went, why God took the baby to heaven and why He wouldn't put it back. I wept silently when my 4yo was saying her nightly prayers and asked God to give her back her baby sibling and to be sure it was a baby brother.

We had recently moved to a new area and knew very few people. I felt alone, no one to share in my heartache. I suffered in silence all weekend and went to the doctors first thing Monday morning where they did blood work, an exam and confirmed what I already knew...the baby was gone. My dearest friend sent me a letter after learning of our loss and she just wrote a few verses of scripture and said that she is crying with me. Another friend from church pulled me aside while her husband pulled mine aside. She pulled me into a deep hug and just wept with me. While she had never experienced a miscarriage before, she knew what it was to lose a baby and to us it was the same. We cried together and she gave me permission (something I had been refusing to acknowledge) to grieve, be sad, be angry, etc... She encouraged me through every emotion to cry out that emotion to God and give it over to Him.

It has been months now...had the baby not left us he/she would be 32 weeks and making his/her debut in just a few short weeks. As the days pass God has given me peace, but the longing is still there, the emptiness is still there - just as it is anytime you lose a love one. The best comfort is knowing that one day...I will see my perfect child again for he/she is waiting for us in Heaven!

~ Ruthann M.

◊ ◊ ◊

Loss at 10-12 Weeks

We had a due date of March 2015 with our 8th child. I always feel sick at around 6 weeks but the sickness never came and I was experiencing bleeding beyond the typical implantation bleeding, which was not normal either. I knew that something was wrong but was hoping for the best.

We went in for an ultrasound, resulting in an empty sac. I miscarried naturally in August and went on to get pregnant right away with a due date on our anniversary in May 2015. We were very hopeful this one would be ok since I had previously had 7 healthy pregnancies with absolutely no complications before the miscarriage in August. I had a small amount of bleeding early in the pregnancy but when we went in for the ultrasound at 10 weeks 3 days we got to see our baby and hear the heartbeat! We were so happy and relieved and I felt like I could finally get excited about our baby.

Two weeks later I went in by myself for what I thought was a normal checkup. Our nurse midwife checked for the heartbeat only to find nothing. She tried three times with different machines and there was nothing. I was shocked and devastated. I cried all the way home and had to tell my husband and children. It was so far the hardest thing I have ever went through. To be able to see and hear my baby and then to have the news that it had passed away before I even got to hold him or her.

I cried a lot but God was faithful. I had been studying Psalm 103 the whole month of November (when everything took place). It was such perfect timing. It is a psalm that I had memorized a couple years before. It talks of praising and blessing the Lord for who He is and "all His benefits". I was able to study and meditate on these truths during the hardest times.

We decided to wait for the miscarriage to take place naturally against their advice to have a D&C. I was scared to have a D&C and wanted to be able to see my baby. I am glad I did. On November 16th our baby was born at home. When I saw the baby for the first time I cried. Soon after I delivered the Lord gave me the name "Judah" for our baby. We found out later that it meant "to praise" or "to thank" which was so neat since that is what the psalm I had been reading and studying was all about!

Everything didn't turn out like I thought it would. We ended up in the hospital having passed out several times because of so much blood loss. Ending with a D&C and lots of fluids, I was finally able to start my recovery physically and emotionally. I have to put in here that when I woke up from the D&C, certain verses on His "benefits" in the psalm went through my head and I was able to receive comfort from that. Praise God!

God also showed me through all of this that I am to desire children for His benefit - not my own. You see, I have always LOVED and desired babies and was thrilled that God was giving us so many but it is not about just having the babies – it's about raising them for the Lord. That they can make a difference for and bring glory to HIM! It has made me cling to God even more and has made a huge difference in my prayer life. My miscarriage is still pretty recent at the time of this testimony so we have not gotten pregnant again yet, but I am ok with whatever God has planned for our family. His will, not mine, be done!

~ Kristina

◊ ◊ ◊

Loss at 8 Weeks

Our story begins with getting married and never thinking we may have difficulties having children. We were married 3 years, and were extremely excited to be finally pregnant! But at 8 short weeks our lives were crushed and we lost our baby. I really couldn't think of anyone that I knew had a miscarriage so I felt alone. We didn't tell anyone for 2 days.

I cried and my husband became "busy" on a house project. It was through communication that we learned what each other needed to heal and get through it. It wasn't that he didn't care; it was his way of working through his own grief, by doing physical work. Talking about it and crying were healing to me. Communication really is the key when going through such a hard time.

Four months later, we lost another tiny baby. I could hardly go shopping without tears welling up, just seeing babies and pregnant women was hard. I became a little distant and closed to prevent being hurt by people who didn't understand how raw their words sounded. My husband would also protect me by quietly standing beside me, depending on whom he saw was talking to me at large gatherings.

On the roller coaster of emotions, I would read Romans 4:20, (Abraham) - "He staggered not at the promise of God through unbelief; but was strong in faith, giving glory to God." I also found comfort reading about all the women in the Bible who were strong, but yet struggled with being barren. We really did feel God wanted us to have children, but something was wrong.

We didn't want to go medical, but after the first loss we did take some tests, which said I was healthy. We went to the Word of God and printed out all the verses about being fruitful and multiplying, being blessed with children, etc. Many people gave us their advice and things we should try. I did a lot of different cleanses, vitamins, etc. But it all seemed like we were "shooting" in the dark.

That's when our pastor's one statement while preaching, literally changed our lives. He said, "If you are praying and praying for something, but nothing is happening, then stop. And ask God for wisdom on why it's not happening." We went home and prayed for wisdom for our situation.

The very next week I came across a website about endometrioses, which I had never heard about before. All the symptoms were what I was experiencing. I changed my diet, etc to heal the endometrioses along with still believing that God would do a miracle work.

A year and half later we were pregnant again and after being married 6 ½ years, our healthy full term baby was born. Looking back, we know that it was God's grace and strength that helped us walk through those tough years. We praise God for our miracle, and remember the ones who are waiting for us in heaven.

~ Louise F.

◊ ◊ ◊

Loss at 8 Weeks

In February 1984, God blessed us with a healthy 9#5oz boy. The pregnancy was wonderful and the delivery normal. I thought, "This is a piece of cake!"

In 1986 we were pregnant again. With no morning sickness, I thought this pregnancy was going to be even easier than the first! But at 7 weeks I started spotting. Then I began having cramps. We were at my in-laws watching a 4th of July special on television, and as the fireworks were bursting over New York Harbor, my insides felt like they were going to burst. I went to the bathroom and when I sat on the toilet, I felt something bigger than normal pass. Something told me it was more than just a huge blood clot, so I fished it out and checked it over.

There in my hand was my precious, tiny baby. It had tiny little eye spots, tiny little arms, and tiny little legs. It was only about an inch long. But it was dead. Why had God given me this baby to only take it away?

We called the doctor to see if he needed to examine the baby, but he told us no. We asked him what should we do with it, and he told us to flush it. That's what we did, and believe me, we've regretted it ever since, but we can't undo what we did. All I could do was cry...and cry...and cry. The moment I knew I was pregnant I was picturing this baby, holding it, thinking of names, fixing up the nursery. But all hopes and dreams for this baby were flushed away.

I'm ashamed to admit that, as a Christian, I did not handle my miscarriage very well; I was angry at God for taking my baby. I did not trust my God to know what was best for me or for the baby, and that He was in control.

When we went for a checkup, my doctor said if I didn't stop crying he would recommend a psychologist. He said there was obviously something wrong and I should be thankful. (I found out later he did abortions, so that might explain his callous attitude towards the death of our baby.) As soon as I was healed, I got pregnant again. But to my dismay, I started spotting again. I could NOT go through another miscarriage. I knew I'd probably go off the deep end if this one died too.

If you are familiar with the Bible story of Samuel the prophet, then you will know from where our prayer came. In our desperation, we got down on our knees and promised the Lord, "If you will give us this baby, we will give it to you to serve you all the days of its life." I immediately had a HOT FIRE start at my head and travel down my body to my toes!!!!! My spotting stopped, and on July 25, 1987, God gave us a healthy 10# 6 1/2oz girl!!! And her heart is totally sold out to the Lord!!

She turned 16 the summer she spent on mission in Bolivia, 18 the summer she spent serving the Lord in India, 19 in Portugal while learning Portuguese before spending 1 1/2 years serving in Portuguese-speaking Angola. She is now in Anchorage, Alaska learning as much as she can as a

Certified Nurse Mid-Wife before heading back onto the mission field wherever God may call her. My story has a happy ending. I'm so thankful for God healing my body and giving me our daughter. I truly believe life begins at conception. And I also believe that my baby went straight from my womb to heaven. I will get to meet him/her one day.

~ Robin

◊ ◊ ◊

Loss at 8 and 10 Weeks

When we married my husband and I both agreed we wanted to have several children. I became pregnant before our first anniversary and although I was excited my husband was not ready for children. This created feelings of ambivalence inside me- desire for a baby but dislike of the lack of acceptance from my husband. I began spotting on a Saturday evening and by Father's Day morning things were getting worse. We ended up at the ER and at 10 weeks our tiny baby was born. My mind will always remember the little body they put in a small container to show me. We are truly and wonderfully made.

Through the process of medical care they found that I am RH negative. I faced the question of whether God was punishing us because we were not both ready for a baby. I also dealt with emotions and grief while my husband went to denial. We didn't tell many people but I still experienced the hurtful comments that it was just a part of life. I remember attending a social event soon after and very little was asked concerning how I am doing. I came to the place of believing I just need to process on my own in silence. I felt the pain and emotions related to seeing babies born about the time I was due and even as the babies grew I'd think that's the size my baby would be. I did come to accept that God had a plan and it wasn't a punishment. I also chose to name my baby, although I never told the name to anyone other than my husband.

From my perspective there seemed to be very little out there in terms of books on the subject and neither were there online options as my story occurred in the late 90's before internet was common. I am glad that in recent years there has been more concern and awareness of the grief a miscarriage brings. I do believe there are still hurtful comments but as a whole, I see people reaching out with an effort to care.

My second miscarriage occurred after 2 full term pregnancies. I was 8 weeks along and began spotting. Since I had had a miscarriage and some minor complications in the last pregnancy they recommended an ultrasound. That appointment was on my birthday. I had previous ultrasounds and so I knew what the image should look like and what showed was more a mass than a baby. I was not surprised when the technician told me there was no life. I went home to spend the next several days on the sofa waiting for nature to continue its course. I again felt like I grieved in silence- almost as if people didn't know how to respond to me. Of course there was the knowledge of the first time and so I tended to be more careful or had fewer expectations of others and their lack.

Several months later we attended some classes that really helped me process everything. I cannot say it never bothered me after that but it began a healing for the emptiness that a miscarriage brings and for the pain I felt in others not caring. It has made me more aware of how to respond to others in the future. I look forward to meeting 2 precious ones in heaven but in the meantime I have a great responsibility to care for the 6 that God has allowed us to keep on earth.

~ Fay D.

◊ ◊ ◊

Loss at 12 Weeks

As my vehicle sped along, the late afternoon sun filtered through the fall leaves and danced on the road ahead. But my eyes weren't on the scenery. Instead, I saw my hands gripping the steering wheel, and my knuckles were white. "Relax!" I told myself. "Everything will be just fine." But deep inside I was already regretting that I had insisted my husband stay home with our eighteen month son, Johann, while I went for my doctor appointment. I had one of my 'feelings'; and I had long ago learned to not ignore those. After all, in spite of my diagnosis with PCOS Johann had been born a mere ten months after our wedding. And the pregnancy and birth had gone off without a hitch, but I still couldn't relax.

It all began on a crisp evening in September. Because of a case of bad timing, for two hours we found ourselves stuck in a parade in our small town. As we sat there and watched the endless procession of every emergency vehicle imaginable, I realized that I felt sick. By the time that last air horn had faded into the distance, I was sure I was pregnant. By the way my tummy and my emotions felt, a pregnancy test was in the very near future.

That night I took a pregnancy test, which showed positive. I experienced an enormous flood of emotions. I wanted more children, but I also wanted more time with the rather difficult son I had. Since his birth, we had faced many challenges. There was colic and allergies. There was heavy teething, colds, fevers, ear infections, and most of all, sleepless nights. Over the next weeks I prayed over my pregnancy and pleaded with God to prepare my heart and arms for the gift he was giving me.

Most days I was too sick to function very well at all. It was a struggle to just stay hydrated. Johann could pull off a great imitation of my vomiting, which greatly amused anyone who saw it. People told me that I was likely having a healthy pregnancy because of the severity of my morning sickness. In spite of their comforting words, I still had a dark, almost ominous feeling about my pregnancy. I could never put my finger on exactly what I was feeling; and neither could I bring myself to tell anyone, not even my husband.

Now, here I was, twelve weeks into my pregnancy, and on the way to my first appointment with my midwife. I was feeling much better. The nausea had marvelously left two weeks earlier, which had surprised me. With my first pregnancy, I hadn't felt better until about fourteen weeks. In spite of the lack of nausea, my heart was still heavy. Somehow I just knew that something wasn't right. As I drove, I committed my life and the life of the child I was carrying to One who had given that life. I pleaded with Him to reveal today what the problem was; I couldn't keep living with this dread of not knowing.

As I lay on the examining table, the midwife told me that by the way my uterus felt, I was definitely pregnant, but she wanted to hear the heartbeat on the Doppler to be sure. She turned on the Doppler and positioned it, then repositioned it, maneuvering it all over my lower abdomen. With each passing second, I was afraid I knew my answer. Helping me sit up, she announced, "I'm going to walk you over to ultrasound, you may have your dates wrong, and the baby is too young to find on the Doppler. I mutely agreed. I was speechless with the knowing that I would never hold my baby. You can't be sick for weeks on end and have a baby too young to find on the Doppler.

The ultrasound proved my fears were right. There was no heartbeat to hear. There was no fluttering of the still tiny arms and legs. Our baby had gone before us. There are no words to describe that feeling. At that moment I had no tears, just a paralyzing shock, and at the same time, an odd sensation of relief, because now I knew. The midwife sent me home with a hug, and a stack of information on the process of miscarriage. "We'll give you a couple weeks before we do a D and C," she told me. As I drove and sobbed my way home, I ran her words through my mind. I wondered how a woman can go on living with death haunting her womb?

Carrying on with life proved to be anything but easy. The lack of closure was very difficult. I didn't like to go anywhere. It just felt so odd to go get groceries with a lifeless baby inside me. It seemed as if carrying on with life was somehow sacrilegious. I found huge amounts of comfort at the feet of Jesus, in the arms of my husband, and in the giggles of my precious son. The arrival of my sister, from out of state, helped my mental and emotional health as well.

Over the course of the next two weeks I swallowed herbs, drank teas, and did lots of strenuous things. I had some spotting and occasional cramping, but nothing that seemed promising. Three weeks after the ultrasound, the midwife gently prodded me in the direction of a D and C. As much as I was determined to deliver this baby myself, even I knew that the lack of closure was getting to me. I was showing sign of depression and anxiety. Being pregnant, yet not pregnant, was so difficult.

A few days later, I went in for a very uneventful D and C. The baby was decomposed to the point that the doctor could not see if it was a boy or a girl. It was the size of an eight week old fetus, but it had probably been behind in growth, and had actually died at ten weeks when my nausea left. I experienced so many ups and downs in the days right after the D and C. I was surprised at the level of anger I felt. I felt so robbed. It seemed that the doctor had taken what was mine, and left me no evidence that the baby had ever existed. I experienced huge hormone swings, mild hot flashes, and dark moods in those days following my D and C. Once again, God and my wonderful husband were my places of refuge. Now, eight weeks later, my hormones have leveled out. I feel like a new person. My life has a new depth in having known the grief of losing a baby.

Every dark place we experience brings a sweeter joy when the sun shines again.

I will always wonder if the baby was a boy or a girl. May 21 will come and go, and no tiny pink or blue clothes will be stacked on the changing table. The magnitude of the loss I feel proves that life is sacred. It proves children are truly a heritage from the Lord. It gives me such peace to know that my baby is with the One who lent him to me for such a short time.

~ Lois Troyer

◊ ◊ ◊

Loss at 13 Weeks

I was almost 14 weeks and feeling great. At age 44 and having endured several early miscarriages, I thought I was home free this time. But not so. One morning I found some slight spotting and tried not to panic. I prayed for the Lord's will to be done but trusted that He could prevent a miscarriage if it was His plan.

Early that afternoon, my water broke, I ran to the toilet, and the baby just basically "fell" out. I was in shock. I had experienced no pain and didn't realize I had been in labor at all. It happened so quickly. My husband helped me retrieve our baby's little body, and we discovered it was a boy...just like we prayed for. I held him in a receiving blanket. I just wanted so badly to give his little life dignity and value in spite of where he'd been born. We let our other 6 children see him, cuddle him (still in the blanket), and said goodbye.

After a call to our midwife, it was clear that I needed to go to the hospital. I didn't want to go, but God knew I was going to need help. Due to heavy bleeding, I might have died if I'd stayed home (we live almost an hour from a hospital or emergency help), and I almost did at the hospital. God in His mercy, surrounded us with prayer warriors, even my nurse in the ER told me she'd been praying for me. While at the hospital, I couldn't sleep. I was still in shock from the loss of the baby.

A sweet nurse asked if we had named the baby. Glad she asked. That got me thinking. I had been praying for some time for another little boy. God heard my prayer. We named our baby Samuel. That was an important step because we wanted to witness to others that every life (short or long) has value in God's eyes and to remind ourselves, as well of God's faithfulness.

We buried our little Samuel in the backyard. The children and I painted some rocks and placed them at the site. My oldest daughter helped set up flowers. It was so good for our children to be able to have a spot to grieve if they needed to, and they did. We told them Samuel's spirit was in heaven with Jesus and that only his body was in the ground. We reminded them (and ourselves) of how happy and whole he was in heaven. It was still difficult to process the loss though.

I wished I knew why it had happened for my own sake, but I wasn't prepared for what an impact it would have on the children. Even my 2 year-old asked daily about the baby in my tummy. I can say now after 3 months, that the sting of the loss has faded, but there is still a deep longing. I can say also that the Lord has helped me to be thankful even in the midst of our great loss...thankful that I could even get pregnant again. This has been a lesson in trusting for our family. Trusting that God is good and that when you can't see His hand - you can still trust His heart (as I heard in a sermon once and a song, too I believe).

~ Noel

For Those Looking On

It was my last pregnancy and I was eight weeks along. Since the previous pregnancy had ended in a miscarriage, I was especially worried. Although I was engulfed in wrenching morning sickness, I still wanted an ultrasound to set my mind at ease. So the appointment was made and I awaited the day.

A few days before going in, a very dear friend of mine asked if she could go with me. Darlene was and is a close friend – one I hope to keep until I'm old and gray. She had been there with me during my previous miscarriage. She had been the one who sat beside me during the church ladies get-togethers when seeing new babies and pregnant ladies was so incredibly hard.

Darlene didn't say much. She didn't have to. Good friends know when the other is hurting, and when to be silent.

We went to the ultrasound and, although it took a few tries, the midwife eventually found the precious little baby – now our 1 ½ year old little guy. Upon getting ready to leave the office, Darlene broke the happy news to me that she was also pregnant! And we were due only two days apart! She wanted to wait to tell me until we had found out whether or not my baby was alive. That has come to mean even more to me as the years pass.

Let me tell you for those looking on – those who have never suffered a miscarriage – **be like my sweet friend.**

I know it is hard when you must be the one watching someone else go through a hard time or loss of any kind. Sometimes the fear that we will say the wrong thing keeps us from saying anything at all.

These are few of things that can mean so much to women who are going through an early miscarriage:

- **Acknowledge that her baby was real.** It wasn't a blob of tissue. It was a person and her heart is grieving deeply for that sweet child.
- **Let her know you care.** It doesn't have to be much, but acknowledge

the grief she is walking through. A simple, silent hug can do wonders for her heart. Tears shed together draws two women together.

- **Don't tell her it is probably best that it died** – that something was most likely wrong with it. This hurts so much. She will come to understand this in time, but in the moment of grief that is hard to comprehend. Use discretion in what you say.

- **Sit with her at gatherings.** You don't have to say anything at all. Sometimes she loves silence. But knowing you are there to be a sort of buffer against the world – even if only for an hour or two – can mean so much to her.

- **If she doesn't answer the phone when you call, don't be offended.** She might be in the middle of a torrent of tears when your call is ringing. Leave a message or text that shows how much you care about her.

- **Give her a gift that says "I love you – even in your pain".** This can be something that you know she finds comfort in.

The sweet ladies who also shared their miscarriage stories with us have given us some pointers to those looking on.

Don't try to encourage them by saying "You'll get pregnant again". Just let her talk! Listen, cry, hug. Don't try to empathize by sharing your miscarriage experience unless she asks. When we stood in front of our church and told them I was miscarrying, the pastor had every couple that had walked through the same get up, surround us and pray over us. We all cried together, it was very, very powerful and even though no one said anything, we knew we weren't alone (2 Cor 1:4).

~ Lacey

One of the older ladies at church sent me a letter saying that she had gone through a miscarriage many years before and that she knew what I was going through. It meant so much. Now I try to write notes to others when I hear of their miscarriage. Drop off flowers even if you don't know what to say. Never say" you can have another baby.

~ Michelle

Be a listening ear. Call the dear friend, and let her talk about her grief. Stop in with a bouquet of flowers, even if it's been years since your little one has passed over on angels wings. A friend remembered our still born son 10th birthday with a basket full of fresh flowers, it meant SO much. Just be there for your friend!

~ Tina Zimmerman

Early miscarriage often leaves no tangible evidence of that precious little life - - no ultrasound photos, no soft blankets or sweet clothes, no memory. Give her the gift of a tangible memory: for example, an angel figurine, a small snuggly blanket embroidered with the due date (and name, if the parents chose one), a small teddy bear, or a pin with tiny footprints on it (available through some crisis pregnancy centers). REMEMBER the due date, and do something special for her on that day. Use your phone or planner to remind yourself of that date for several years, because believe me, she won't forget it; and it will mean the world to her heart if someone else remembers with her. If you don't know what to say, say only this: "I'm so sorry, and I care."

~ Joanna Yoder

My biggest advice for helping a friend through a miscarriage is to allow and validate her grief. Don't try to sugarcoat the situation. I had comments made like "it's probably for the best..you could have had a very sick baby" and those kinds of comments aren't helpful at all. Everyone grieves differently and there is no time limit for true grief. Just be there for her and acknowledge the life that's been lost.

~ Savannah Berniquez

The way I got through my three losses was to plant my favor color rose and to dedicate it to my baby. I also went to a website called Calvin's Hats where they send women who have lost babies little crocheted hats. It truly helped me with my memorializing part. Family and friends helped with the part of talking to someone and voicing my feelings and the pain I was in. I was told that there is always light at the end of the tunnel and no matter how hard things seem to be that you'll get through them. There was a sweet poem that a friend had sent me and it went: "An angel in the book of Life, wrote down my child's birth, and as he closed the book he whispered 'Too beautiful for earth'." I truly believe this and I go by it every single day.

~ Racheal Heath

Accept the loss of a baby as just that, the death of a loved one. Hug tightly and cry alongside them. Search the Scriptures for some comforting verses like: Psalm 139: 14, 17; Philippians 4:4, 11; Philippians 4:13; Philippians 4: 19. Remind them that husbands grieve differently as they experience pregnancy differently. Remind them of the beautiful fact that their baby is in the loving arms of Jesus, awaiting them, in Heaven!

~ Ruthann M.

Give the momma a special "pamper herself" gift to show you care. Or a meal is always a thoughtful gesture. Know what the momma wants. Some ladies want to talk about their story to others; some would rather keep it to themselves and think being "questioned" is rude. (My sister and I are opposites in this area when we both went thru losses. If you have never went thru a loss, its ok to just give a hug and say "I'm sorry for your loss."

~ Louise F.

You are not alone. So many understanding women from my church shared their miscarriage experiences upon hearing of mine. So now I can comfort others with the comfort that I received. I personally know some of your pain. Forgive people when they say, "You can just have another one" or "There must have been something wrong with it, so be thankful." Know that your child is in heaven. (2 Samuel 12:22-23) Know that God loves you and is not punishing you. Know that God is in control; trust Him.

~ Robin

Bring a meal or other food items. Take small children home with you for an hour or two so the mother can rest. Allow them to share their experience and the things they are facing. Pray for them and tell them you are doing so. Remember the due date and call them or send a card near that time. Offer to help with gardening, cleaning or any other job that needs done.

~ Fay D.

All I can say is don't lose faith and don't lose sight of God. I found that through those tough times it's easy to forget that when it feels like you're alone you never really are. God said, "I will never leave you nor forsake you." Also, it's easy to be angry and want to isolate yourself, believe me I know that first hand, but try not to let that happen. Sometimes people said things that I thought were silly and downright mean but they did not mean it in that way. One comment that made me angry was "If God wants you to have a baby, you will". Boy did that comment heat me up! I would respond "Oh and those crack babies that were left in the dumpster to die, oh God wanted that huh?!" I'd tell them not to say those dumb things to me since it made me think of all of those poor babies that were born in horrible conditions and I knew it wouldn't be that way for a baby born into a family that I know God wants to bless.

~ Melissa Cummins

My advice to friends of miscarriage survivors is to give your friend a big hug, tell them you love them and are praying for them, and even to cry with them. Cards are lovely too. One card I got was so beautiful that I will always cherish the caption, "With God there are no endings, just beginnings." I had a friend bring some food and her children, so that we could all find a little joy and comfort for a day in the midst of our grieving. Some friends brought us groceries and a lovely potted flower that could be planted. Another sent us a flower bush. That was excellent because we can add them to the little garden where the baby is buried. A church ministered to me by giving me a cup with a floral arrangement in it. All these visual reminders help me so much to remember little Samuel. People sharing their story of loss has also been helpful to me. I would also say that what was not helpful was anyone saying this, "Something must have been wrong with the baby." That could very well be true, but at least for me that made my precious lost baby sound like a problem not a person.

~ Noel

Grieving Silently No Longer

"And God shall wipe away all tears from their eyes; and there shall be no more death, neither sorrow, nor crying, neither shall there be any more pain: for the former things are passed away.

And He that sat upon the throne said, Behold, I make all things new. And He said unto me, Write: for these words are true and faithful.

And He said unto me, It is done. I am Alpha and Omega, the beginning and the end. I will give unto him that is athirst of the fountain of the water of life freely.

He that overcometh shall inherit all
things; and I will be his God, and he shall be my
son." Revelation 21:4-7

Coming through a miscarriage can have an enormous effect on you. I know. I've been there.

As we each face the valley of death in losing a child, we come upon this question: how are we going to let this circumstance change us? Because it most definitely will change us – either for better or worse.

I am going to leave you with a few reminders on how to take our heartbreak and circumstances - and turn them into something that God could use for His honor and His glory.

Cling to the Lord and Savior Jesus Christ. If you are not already a born-again Christian, then you first need to realize you are a sinner, repent of your sin, fall on your knees before God Himself, and ask for His forgiveness and make Him Lord of your life. Once you have done that, cling to Him through this miscarriage – drinking of the water of life freely. Think of it like one of those sticky weeds that cling to your clothes and are hard to peel off. Tell Him "Lord, You are the one who allowed this to happen, and I am in this for the long haul. I will be here as You get me through this heartbreak."

Refuse to become bitter. Bitterness can eat a person from the inside out. It not only affects you, but it also greatly affects those you come in contact with – especially your family. Bitterness is sin and needs to be confessed as such. Instead, allow this heartbreak to drive you to the Lord. Allow Him to mold your heart into something soft and pliable for His use. Let Him pick up the shattered pieces of your heart and make you beautiful within!

Believe that God can make something good of this circumstance. *"And we know that all things work together for good to them that love God, to them who are the called according to His purpose."* Romans 8:28 It might look like this valley is too deep, too dark, and too long for anything good to come of it. But remember that what we call good is not always what God calls good. He has our souls in mind, not our earthly happiness.

Grasp the fact that God has a purpose. I am the kind of person that likes to intellectually understand where I am headed and why I am headed there. In the midst of grief, there is no understanding of direction whatsoever. After much struggle, I finally came to the place where I could say "Lord, I have no idea what Your plan is – but I am going to believe You have one." It was a broken, yet freeing moment for me. I had stepped out in faith. And that's really all God wanted.

<u>Allow God to use your pain for His glory.</u> It goes against our human reasoning to believe that my pain may somehow help your pain – but when did God ever use human reasoning? My husband once told our congregation: "When hurting people ask for prayer and help . . . it's very possible their answer to prayer is you." We cannot help in the divine, sovereign way God can, but we can be His hands and feet on earth. You and your walk through grief might be the answer to someone else's cry for help. Let God use you.

Finally . . .

lift your eyes heavenward and
watch for the glorious coming of
the King of kings and Lord of
lords.

Someday these tears will be
remembered no more.

About the Author

Living in northern Idaho, Kendra Graber is the wife to Lowell, and a mom to five ornery, lovable boys and one sweet girl. Some of her favorite things are caramel lattes, slobbery baby kisses, flirty texts from her husband, and flowerbeds full of petunias.

If she is not cooking, cleaning, running errands or doing laundry, she can be found in one of her favorite places: her garden. To find out more about her life and beliefs, you can visit her blog at www.livingintheshoe.com.

Above all, her purpose in life is to hold up the name of the One who saved her from her sins, the Lord Jesus Christ.

For orders, contact publisher at:

Truth in Word Publishing, LLC

1444 Homestead Loop

Bonners Ferry, ID 83805

www.truthinwordpublishing.com

CPSIA information can be obtained
at www.ICGtesting.com
Printed in the USA
FSOW02n1153200917
38984FS